Blockchain Technology in Shipping: Improving Transparency and Efficiency

Table of Contents

Preface

Introduction

Prelude

Chapter 1: Basics of Blockchain Technology

Chapter 2: Challenges in the Shipping Industry

Chapter 3: How Blockchain Can Improve Transparency in Shipping

Chapter 4: How Blockchain Can Improve Efficiency in Shipping

Chapter 5: Real-World Applications of Blockchain in Shipping

Chapter 6: Challenges and Limitations of Blockchain in Shipping

Conclusion

Glossary

Preface

The **maritime and shipping industries** are undergoing profound changes, driven by **technological advancements**, stricter **regulatory frameworks**, and an increasing demand for **efficiency and transparency** in global trade. Blockchain technology is emerging as a powerful solution to many of the challenges faced by the shipping sector, offering a decentralized and secure method for improving **data management, supply chain visibility**, and **operational efficiency**. In response to these industry needs, the **Gosships Learning Series** was developed to provide professionals with practical, accessible knowledge on how to navigate this new technological landscape.

This series is designed to provide **foundational to intermediate knowledge** on blockchain technology, with a focus on **practical applications** and real-world relevance to the shipping industry. Each book is paired with a **certification test**, ensuring that the knowledge gained is not only understood but can also be effectively applied in professional settings.

The **Gosships Learning Series** aims to empower maritime and shipping personnel, from **entry-level crew members** to **shoreside managers**, by equipping them with the skills necessary to adopt blockchain solutions in their operations. We believe this series will support your professional growth and open new opportunities for success in the ever-evolving maritime industry.

Introduction

Welcome to the **Gosships Learning Series**, designed for professionals looking to **expand their knowledge** and enhance their careers in the maritime and shipping sectors. This book, titled *"Blockchain Technology in Shipping: Improving Transparency and Efficiency"*, was meticulously crafted by industry experts, ensuring that the content is both **authoritative** and aligned with the latest **industry standards**. Whether you are new to the topic or seeking to deepen your expertise, this resource will provide you with the insights needed to implement blockchain solutions and contribute to more **transparent**, **efficient**, and **secure** shipping operations.

In this book, we will explore the following key areas:

- **Blockchain Fundamentals in Shipping**: Understand how blockchain technology works and its potential applications within the shipping industry.

- **Smart Contracts**: Learn how smart contracts can automate processes, reduce paperwork, and enhance trust between stakeholders.

- **Supply Chain Transparency**: Discover how blockchain enables real-time tracking of shipments, ensuring greater accountability and reducing fraud.

- **Sustainability and Compliance**: Explore how blockchain can help monitor **carbon emissions**, track **environmental compliance**, and support sustainability efforts.

- **Challenges and Future Trends**: Gain insights into the current barriers to blockchain adoption, such as **regulatory issues**, and learn about future trends shaping the industry.

After completing this book, you will be ready to take an **assessment** designed to test your comprehension of the material. Upon successful completion of the assessment, you can obtain a **Certificate of Achievement** by visiting **www.gosships.com** and accessing the training platform. This certificate will validate your expertise in blockchain technology and its applications in the shipping industry, demonstrating your proficiency to peers and industry leaders.

Who is this book for?

This book is designed for:

- **Maritime and shipping personnel** seeking to understand and implement blockchain technology in their operations.

- **Shoreside managers** looking to enhance their knowledge of blockchain's role in improving operational efficiency and supply chain transparency.

- **Aspiring students** aiming to enter the shipping industry with a solid foundation in cutting-edge technology and digital solutions.

- **Government and regulatory personnel** interested in staying informed about the evolving standards and best practices surrounding blockchain adoption in global trade.

By mastering the concepts covered in this book, you will be equipped to help your organization navigate the **complexities of modern shipping**, stay compliant with **international regulations**, and contribute to a safer, more transparent, and efficient global supply chain.

Thank you for choosing the **Gosships Learning Series** to support your journey of continuous learning and professional growth in the rapidly advancing field of **Blockchain Technology in Shipping**.

Gosships Learning Series 2024/2025

1. Hydrogen: The Fuel of the Future
2. Green Ammonia: The Next Big Thing in Shipping
3. Decarbonizing Shipping: Pathways to Zero Emissions
4. Battery Technology for Industrial Applications
5. Carbon Capture and Storage: Can It Save the Planet?
6. Biofuels 101: Turning Waste into Energy
7. Understanding LNG (Liquefied Natural Gas)
8. Methanol as a Marine Fuel
9. Offshore Wind Energy: The Future of Renewable Power
10. Tidal and Wave Energy: Harnessing the Ocean
11. Electrofuels: The Next Generation of Carbon-Neutral Fuels
12. Energy Storage Systems for Grid Reliability
13. Hydrogen Fuel Cells for Transportation
14. Solar Energy Innovations: Beyond Solar Panels
15. Smart Grids: The Backbone of Future Energy Systems
16. Ammonia-Hydrogen Blends: A Dual Fuel Solution?
17. Nuclear Power: Small Modular Reactors for a Low-Carbon Future
18. Hydropower: The Oldest Renewable Energy Source
19. Decentralized Energy Systems: Microgrids for Resilience
20. Energy Efficiency Technologies for Industry
21. Hydrogen Production from Seawater
22. Fuel Cells for Maritime Applications
23. Geothermal Energy: Unlocking Earth's Heat
24. Future of EV Charging Infrastructure
25. Synthetic Fuels: Bridging the Gap to Decarbonization
26. Cybersecurity for Maritime and Offshore Operations

27	AI and Automation in Shipping and Logistics
28	Digital Twins in Maritime: Revolutionizing Asset Management
29	Risk Management in Offshore and Maritime Operations
30	Compliance with IMO 2020 Regulations
31	Sustainable Ship Design: Reducing Environmental Impact
32	Marine Renewable Energy: Wave, Tidal, and Offshore Wind Integration
33	Ballast Water Management Systems
34	Blockchain Technology in Shipping: Improving Transpc'y & Efficiency
35	Effective Supply Chain Management for Energy Industries
36	Leadership in the Energy Transition
37	Effective Crisis Management in Maritime Operations
38	Shipyard Safety Management Systems
39	Port State Control (PSC) Inspection Readiness
40	Remote Vessel Operations and Autonomous Shipping
41	Optimizing Fleet Performance with Data Analytics
42	Maritime Environmental Regulations: Staying Ahead of Compliance
43	Advanced Maintenance Strategies: Condition Monitoring & Predictive Maintenance
44	Global LNG Market: Trends and Opportunities
45	Incident Investigation in Maritime Operations
46	International Maritime Law: Key Concepts and Applications
47	Emergency Preparedness and Response for Offshore Oil & Gas
48	Energy Transition Strategies for Oil and Gas Companies
49	Maritime Drones: Applications and Safety Considerations
50	Effective Project Management in Offshore Energy Projects

All Rights Reserved Disclaimer

The contents of this book, including but not limited to all text, graphics, images, logos, and designs, are the intellectual property of Gosships LLC and are protected by copyright law. No part of this publication may be reproduced, distributed, transmitted, displayed, or modified in any form or by any means, including photocopying, recording, or other electronic or mechanical methods, without the prior written permission of the publisher, except in the case of brief quotations in critical reviews or articles.

The information contained within this book is for educational purposes only and is provided "as is" without warranty of any kind, either expressed or implied. The authors and publishers disclaim any liability for any direct, indirect, or consequential loss or damage arising from the use of the material in this book.

For permissions or inquiries, please contact: admin@gosships.com

© 2024 Gosships LLC. All rights reserved.

Prelude

The shipping industry is the lifeblood of global trade, transporting approximately 80% of the world's goods across oceans. However, despite its essential role, the industry is riddled with challenges that impede efficiency and hinder transparency. Complex supply chains involve multiple stakeholders, fragmented communication channels, and an overwhelming amount of paperwork. Fraud, tampering, and human errors add to the burden, resulting in delays, increased costs, and disputes.

In this digital era, blockchain technology offers a revolutionary solution to the long-standing inefficiencies in shipping. Known for its decentralized and immutable nature, blockchain provides an opportunity to enhance transparency, traceability, and accountability in shipping operations. By using distributed ledgers, stakeholders can access real-time, verifiable information while automating processes through smart contracts. This book delves into how blockchain is transforming the shipping industry by improving both transparency and efficiency.

Whether you're a shipping professional, a technology enthusiast, or a beginner looking to understand the basics of blockchain, this book will guide you through the key concepts, real-world applications, and challenges of integrating blockchain into the shipping ecosystem.

Chapter 1
Basics of Blockchain Technology

To understand blockchain's impact on shipping, it is essential to grasp the fundamental principles behind the technology. Blockchain is often described as a distributed ledger technology (DLT) where transactions are recorded in blocks, linked in a chain, and maintained by multiple nodes (computers) across a network. This decentralized structure ensures that no single party controls the ledger, making the system transparent, tamper-proof, and highly secure.

What is Blockchain?

Blockchain technology is a digital ledger that records transactions across several computers in such a way that the recorded information cannot be altered retroactively. Blockchain operates on three core principles:

- **Decentralization**: Unlike traditional databases, which are centralized and controlled by a single entity, blockchain operates on a decentralized network where every participant holds a copy of the ledger.

- **Transparency**: Each participant can view the transactions recorded on the blockchain. However, the data is encrypted, ensuring privacy while maintaining transparency for authorized users.

- **Immutability**: Once data is recorded in a block, it cannot be altered or deleted, providing a permanent and auditable record.

Chart 1: Key Characteristics of Blockchain

Feature	Description
Decentralization	Data is shared across a distributed network
Transparency	All authorized users have visibility into the data
Immutability	Data cannot be altered or tampered with

How Blockchain Works

Blockchain operates through a series of steps that ensure data integrity and security:

1. **Transaction Creation**: A transaction is initiated by a user and broadcast to the network.

2. **Validation**: Nodes in the network use a consensus mechanism (e.g., Proof of Work, Proof of Stake) to validate the transaction.

3. **Block Formation**: Once validated, the transaction is grouped into a block with other transactions.

4. **Chaining Blocks**: Each block contains a cryptographic hash of the previous block, creating an unbreakable chain.

5. **Finalization**: The block is added to the blockchain, and the transaction is completed.

Smart contracts, a key feature of blockchain, are self-executing contracts where the terms are written directly into code. They automatically trigger actions (e.g., payments, shipment releases) when predefined conditions are met, reducing the need for intermediaries and enhancing efficiency.

Chapter 2
Challenges in the Shipping Industry

The shipping industry, despite its critical role in global trade, faces several challenges that hinder its operational efficiency and transparency. These challenges are deeply rooted in the traditional, paper-based processes and fragmented communication systems that are still prevalent today.

Complexity of Global Supply Chains

Global supply chains are inherently complex, involving multiple stakeholders such as carriers, freight forwarders, customs authorities, insurers, and ports. Each of these stakeholders uses different systems and processes to manage their part of the supply chain. The lack of a unified platform results in disconnected information silos, leading to delays and inefficiencies. For instance, the need for numerous handoffs between parties—such as the exchange of bills of lading—introduces delays and increases the likelihood of errors.

Lack of Transparency and Trust Issues

One of the most pressing challenges in shipping is the lack of transparency. With so many intermediaries involved in the movement of goods, it becomes difficult to track the real-time status of shipments. This lack of visibility makes it challenging to identify where delays occur or to verify the authenticity of documents. Moreover, the shipping industry is vulnerable to fraud and tampering, with counterfeit goods often making their way into the supply chain.

Inefficiencies in Shipping

Administrative inefficiencies plague the shipping industry, as much of the documentation—such as bills of lading, customs forms, and invoices—is still processed manually. This reliance on paper-based processes leads to increased costs, delays in communication, and a higher risk of human errors. Shipping delays are often caused by miscommunication between stakeholders, missed paperwork, or regulatory holdups at customs.

Chart 2: Common Inefficiencies in Shipping

Inefficiency	Impact on Shipping
Manual Paperwork	Increased processing times and errors
Fragmented Systems	Lack of real-time tracking and visibility
Disconnected Stakeholders	Delays in communication and decision-making

Chapter 3
How Blockchain Can Improve Transparency in Shipping

Blockchain technology offers a transformative solution to the transparency issues that plague the shipping industry. By providing a single source of truth for all participants, blockchain ensures that all stakeholders have access to the same real-time data, reducing disputes and fostering trust.

Blockchain as a Single Source of Truth

One of blockchain's greatest strengths is its ability to act as a single source of truth. Because the ledger is distributed across multiple nodes, every participant has access to the same information, eliminating discrepancies between stakeholders. This transparency ensures that data—such as shipment status, customs clearance, and transaction records—remains consistent and verifiable by all parties.

Tracking Shipments with Blockchain

The transparency provided by blockchain enables end-to-end visibility of shipments as they move through the supply chain. Each time a product moves from one stage to another (e.g., from manufacturer to carrier to port), the transaction is recorded on the blockchain. This allows stakeholders to track the status of shipments in real time, reducing the risk of lost or stolen goods.

For example, blockchain can be used to track the origin of goods, ensuring that they are sourced from legitimate suppliers. This feature is particularly valuable for industries with high-value goods, such as luxury brands, pharmaceuticals, and electronics, where counterfeit products can cause significant financial losses.

Chart 3: Benefits of Blockchain for Transparency in Shipping

Benefit	Impact on Shipping
Real-time tracking	Increased visibility and reduced risk of theft
Immutable records	Eliminates disputes over shipment status
Fraud prevention	Ensures authenticity of goods and documents

Smart Contracts for Automated Trust

Blockchain's use of smart contracts automates trust between stakeholders by enabling self-executing agreements. For example, a smart contract can be programmed to automatically release payment to a shipping company once goods are delivered to a port and verified by customs authorities. This reduces the need for intermediaries, speeds up transactions, and ensures that parties adhere to the terms of their contracts.

Chapter 4
How Blockchain Can Improve Efficiency in Shipping

In addition to improving transparency, blockchain can significantly enhance the efficiency of shipping operations by automating processes and reducing administrative burdens.

Eliminating Paperwork and Reducing Administrative Burdens

One of the key benefits of blockchain is its ability to digitize and automate the flow of documents. Traditionally, the shipping industry relies on paper-based processes for crucial documents like bills of lading, invoices, and customs declarations. Blockchain enables these documents to be digitized and securely stored on a distributed ledger, reducing the time and cost associated with manual paperwork.

For example, a digital bill of lading stored on the blockchain can be accessed by all relevant parties (shipper, carrier, consignee) in real time, eliminating the need for physical document exchanges and reducing delays in customs clearance.

Streamlining Customs and Port Operations

Blockchain can also improve the efficiency of customs and port operations by automating the exchange of verified digital documents. When a shipment arrives at a port, customs authorities can access real-time information about the cargo, verify its contents against shipping manifests, and approve clearance faster. This reduces the risk of delays caused by missing or inaccurate paperwork.

Optimizing Supply Chain Management with Smart Contracts

Smart contracts can automate a wide range of supply chain processes, from triggering payments to releasing shipments and enforcing compliance checks. For instance, a smart contract can be programmed to release payment automatically once goods have been delivered and verified, reducing the need for manual invoicing and reconciliation.

Chart 4: Efficiency Gains from Blockchain in Shipping

Process	Efficiency Improvement
Paperwork Automation	Reduces delays and human errors
Customs Clearance	Faster processing through real-time verification
Supply Chain Payments	Automated payments reduce reconciliation times

Chapter 5

Real-World Applications of Blockchain in Shipping

Blockchain is no longer a theoretical concept—it is already being applied in the shipping industry, with several companies and consortiums leading the way in blockchain adoption.

Maersk and IBM's TradeLens Platform

One of the most notable blockchain initiatives in shipping is the TradeLens platform, developed by Maersk and IBM. TradeLens is a blockchain-based solution designed to improve data sharing and collaboration across the global shipping industry. By providing a single platform for all supply chain participants, TradeLens enhances transparency, reduces delays, and improves operational efficiency.

Case Study: Improved Customs Clearance with TradeLens

TradeLens has been successfully used by customs authorities in multiple countries to streamline the clearance process. By providing real-time access to shipping documents, TradeLens reduces the time needed to verify cargo and approve clearance, resulting in faster shipment processing.

Blockchain in Freight Forwarding and Cargo Tracking

Several freight forwarding companies are using blockchain to improve cargo tracking and document management. By recording each step of a shipment's journey on the blockchain, these companies can provide their customers with real-time updates on the status of their cargo, improving trust and reducing the risk of disputes.

Other Applications: Blockchain in Insurance and Sustainability

Blockchain is also being used in other areas of the maritime industry, including insurance and sustainability. For example, blockchain-based platforms are being developed to streamline the process of insuring cargo, ensuring that claims are processed quickly and accurately. Additionally, blockchain is being used to track the environmental impact of shipping operations, helping companies reduce their carbon footprint and comply with environmental regulations.

Chapter 6
Challenges and Limitations of Blockchain in Shipping

Despite its potential, blockchain faces several challenges and limitations in the shipping industry that must be addressed before widespread adoption can occur.

Scalability Issues

Blockchain networks, especially public blockchains, face scalability challenges due to the time and resources required to process and validate transactions. In a high-volume industry like shipping, where thousands of transactions occur every day, blockchain networks may struggle to keep up. Solutions such as sidechains, Layer 2 technologies, and alternative consensus mechanisms are being explored to address these scalability issues.

Integration with Existing Systems

Most shipping companies still rely on legacy systems for managing their operations. Integrating blockchain with these existing systems can be complex and costly. Companies must invest in the necessary infrastructure and technical expertise to ensure a smooth transition to blockchain-based platforms.

Regulatory and Legal Challenges

The legal and regulatory landscape surrounding blockchain is still evolving. While blockchain-based documents (such as digital bills of lading) are legally recognized in some jurisdictions, others may not yet accept them as valid. This creates uncertainty for companies that want to adopt blockchain but must navigate varying regulatory requirements.

Chart 5: Challenges of Blockchain Adoption in Shipping

Challenge	Impact on Shipping Industry
Scalability Issues	Limits transaction processing capacity
Integration with Legacy Systems	Increases complexity and cost of adoption
Regulatory Uncertainty	Creates legal challenges in document validity

Chapter 7
The Future of Blockchain in Shipping

Blockchain technology is poised to transform the shipping industry by offering a decentralized, secure, and efficient way to manage data, track assets, and automate processes. Although there are challenges related to scalability, regulation, and integration, the future of blockchain in shipping is bright. Emerging trends in blockchain technology, combined with industry collaboration, are paving the way for broader adoption, improved efficiency, and enhanced sustainability in the maritime sector.

Emerging Trends in Blockchain Technology

One of the most **exciting trends** in blockchain technology is the rise of **decentralized finance (DeFi)** and the **tokenization** of shipping assets. Tokenization refers to the process of representing physical assets, such as ships, cargo, or fuel, as **digital tokens** on a blockchain platform. These tokens can be bought, sold, or traded, providing new avenues for **financing and asset management** within the shipping industry. For example, shipping companies can tokenize their vessels, enabling investors to purchase fractional ownership, thereby democratizing access to shipping investments. Similarly, cargo or fuel can be tokenized, allowing for real-time tracking and more efficient trading processes.

Tokenization also facilitates the **creation of new business models** by making it easier to transfer ownership or manage assets digitally. This shift toward digital asset management could lead to **greater liquidity** in shipping markets and new ways of optimizing shipping operations.

Additionally, **interoperability** between different blockchain platforms is gaining momentum as a key area of focus. The shipping industry consists of numerous stakeholders—ports, carriers, customs, freight forwarders, and regulatory bodies—each using their own platforms and systems. **Interoperable blockchains** would enable these parties to seamlessly share data and information across platforms without data silos. This would significantly improve **collaboration** and reduce **fragmentation** in the shipping industry, fostering a more integrated and transparent supply chain.

Blockchain for Sustainability

Beyond improving efficiency, blockchain is also set to play a significant role in the **sustainability** efforts of the shipping industry. The global maritime sector is under increasing pressure to reduce its **carbon emissions** and contribute to global sustainability goals. Blockchain technology can be used to track **carbon emissions** and **fuel consumption** in real-time, providing companies with valuable data to monitor and reduce their environmental impact. Shipping companies can use this data to ensure compliance with **international environmental regulations**, such as the **International Maritime Organization's (IMO)** emission reduction targets.

Blockchain's ability to ensure **transparency** and **accountability** also makes it a powerful tool for promoting **sustainable practices** across the supply chain. For example, blockchain can be used to track the sourcing, production, and transportation of goods, supporting **circular economy** initiatives by ensuring that materials used in manufacturing and shipping are traceable and sustainably sourced. This traceability is crucial for reducing waste, promoting recycling, and ensuring that products comply with **environmental standards**.

Additionally, blockchain could support the development of **green financing mechanisms** for the shipping industry. By tokenizing carbon credits or creating blockchain-based incentives for companies that adopt greener practices, blockchain technology could help accelerate the shift toward more sustainable shipping operations.

Widespread Adoption and Industry Collaboration

The adoption of blockchain technology in shipping is not happening in isolation. It is driven by **industry collaboration** and support from **key organizations** that recognize its potential to revolutionize maritime operations. **Initiatives such as the Blockchain in Transport Alliance (BiTA)** and the **Digital Container Shipping Association (DCSA)** are bringing together major stakeholders in the shipping and logistics sectors to develop **standards** and **best practices** for blockchain implementation. These collaborations aim to establish **uniform protocols** that ensure blockchain systems are secure, scalable, and interoperable across the global supply chain.

Major companies such as **Maersk** and **IBM** have already launched **blockchain-based solutions** to enhance transparency and efficiency in global trade. For instance, their joint venture, **TradeLens**, provides a secure platform for exchanging shipping documents and tracking containers in real-time, significantly reducing paperwork and improving the speed of cargo clearance at ports. As more companies recognize the benefits of blockchain technology, industry-wide adoption is expected to accelerate, driving further innovation and improvements in shipping operations.

Furthermore, **government regulators** are beginning to explore how blockchain can be integrated into **customs procedures**, cargo inspections, and documentation processes. This regulatory interest is key to ensuring that blockchain solutions can be adopted at a global scale while meeting international legal and safety standards. As blockchain regulations evolve, they will provide the clarity and certainty needed for broader industry adoption.

Conclusion

Blockchain technology offers a **transformative solution** to many of the long-standing challenges facing the shipping industry, including issues related to **transparency, efficiency,** and **data security**. By providing a **decentralized** and **secure platform** for tracking shipments, automating contracts through **smart contracts**, and reducing administrative burdens, blockchain has the potential to **revolutionize global trade**.

The growing interest in **tokenization**, interoperability, and sustainable practices highlights the potential of blockchain to reshape the shipping industry. Blockchain's ability to reduce **carbon emissions**, track environmental impacts, and streamline operations will make it an increasingly important tool for shipping companies seeking to meet **sustainability goals** and remain competitive in a fast-changing global market.

While challenges such as **scalability, integration,** and **regulatory uncertainty** remain, the increasing adoption of blockchain by industry leaders like **Maersk** and **IBM** demonstrates that blockchain is not just a passing trend. As **blockchain technology continues to evolve**, it will become an integral part of shipping and logistics, driving **efficiency, sustainability**, and **innovation** across the maritime sector.

The future of blockchain in shipping is promising, and as industry collaboration continues to grow, blockchain will undoubtedly play a pivotal role in shaping the future of global maritime trade.

Glossary: Blockchain Technology in Shipping: Improving Transparency and Efficiency

1. **Asset Tokenization**: The process of representing physical assets, like ships or cargo, as digital tokens on a blockchain, facilitating ownership transfer and improved asset management.

2. **BiTA (Blockchain in Transport Alliance)**: A group of companies and experts developing blockchain standards for transport and shipping.

3. **Blockchain**: A decentralized digital ledger that records transactions across many computers, ensuring transparency, security, and traceability.

4. **Cargo Tracking**: The ability to monitor the movement of goods in real-time using blockchain, increasing transparency in the shipping supply chain.

5. **Consensus Mechanism**: A protocol used in blockchain to agree on the state of the network and verify transactions, ensuring data integrity.

6. **Cryptographic Hash**: A unique string generated from transaction data that ensures security and data integrity in blockchain technology.

7. **Decentralization**: A key feature of blockchain where no single entity controls the entire network, enhancing security and reducing the risk of fraud.

8. **DeFi (Decentralized Finance)**: Financial applications built on blockchain technology, allowing for transparent and accessible shipping finance solutions.

9. **Digital Container Shipping Association (DCSA)**: A nonprofit group working to standardize digital shipping practices, including blockchain adoption in container shipping.

10. **Distributed Ledger Technology (DLT)**: The technology behind blockchain, where data is distributed across multiple nodes rather than centralized.

11. **Efficiency**: The increased operational effectiveness in shipping achieved through automated processes and real-time tracking via blockchain.

12. **Encryption**: The process of converting data into code to prevent unauthorized access, essential in securing blockchain transactions in shipping.

13. **Ethereum**: A blockchain platform widely used for creating smart

contracts and decentralized applications, with applications in shipping.

14. **Immutability**: A key feature of blockchain where once data is written to the ledger, it cannot be altered or deleted, ensuring transparency and trust.

15. **Interoperability**: The ability for different blockchain systems and platforms to share and exchange data seamlessly, enhancing collaboration in shipping.

16. **IoT (Internet of Things)**: A network of connected devices that can interact and exchange data, often integrated with blockchain for real-time shipping monitoring.

17. **KYC (Know Your Customer)**: A verification process used in blockchain to ensure the identity of users, especially in shipping transactions and regulatory compliance.

18. **Ledger**: A record of transactions in a blockchain network, providing a transparent and secure account of shipping operations.

19. **Maersk**: A leading shipping company that has adopted blockchain technology, notably through its partnership with IBM on the TradeLens platform.

20. **Mining**: The process of verifying transactions and adding them to the blockchain ledger, typically used in public blockchains.

21. **NFT (Non-Fungible Token)**: A unique digital asset stored on a blockchain, potentially used for tracking ownership of rare or valuable goods in shipping.

22. **P2P (Peer-to-Peer)**: A decentralized network model where participants interact directly without intermediaries, commonly used in blockchain shipping systems.

23. **Private Blockchain**: A blockchain network where access is restricted to selected participants, often used for secure shipping and logistics operations.

24. **Public Blockchain**: A decentralized blockchain where anyone can participate, commonly used for transparent shipping processes and supply chain tracking.

25. **Real-Time Data**: Up-to-date information available instantly via blockchain, improving decision-making and visibility in shipping operations.

26. **Regulatory Compliance**: Adhering to industry laws and regulations,

which blockchain helps facilitate by providing a transparent, immutable record of transactions.

27. **SCM (Supply Chain Management)**: The management of the flow of goods from production to delivery, where blockchain improves efficiency and transparency.

28. **Scalability**: The ability of a blockchain network to handle increasing transaction volumes, a challenge for widespread blockchain adoption in shipping.

29. **Secure Ledger**: A blockchain-based ledger that ensures transactions in shipping are recorded in a tamper-proof, encrypted environment.

30. **Smart Contract**: A self-executing contract with the terms directly written into code, automating processes like payments and shipments in the shipping industry.

31. **Stakeholders**: All parties involved in a blockchain-based shipping transaction, including shippers, carriers, freight forwarders, and customs officials.

32. **Supply Chain Transparency**: The ability to track every step of the supply chain, from production to final delivery, using blockchain for better accountability.

33. **Sustainability**: The use of blockchain to monitor and reduce carbon footprints in shipping operations, promoting environmentally friendly practices.

34. **Tamper-Proof**: A key feature of blockchain ensuring that recorded data cannot be altered, crucial for securing shipping transaction records.

35. **Token**: A digital representation of assets or rights that can be traded on a blockchain, such as cargo or fuel in the shipping industry.

36. **Trade Finance**: Financial services supporting international trade, where blockchain can streamline processes like letters of credit and payments.

37. **TradeLens**: A blockchain-based platform developed by Maersk and IBM to provide end-to-end supply chain visibility and transparency.

38. **Transparency**: The clear, traceable nature of blockchain, providing all stakeholders with real-time access to accurate shipping information.

39. **Trustless**: A blockchain concept where transactions occur without the need for intermediaries, enhancing security and reducing fraud in shipping.

40. **Validation**: The process of confirming transactions on a blockchain network, ensuring that shipping data is accurate and authorized.

41. **Verified Gross Mass (VGM)**: A shipping requirement for container weight verification, which blockchain can help automate and record accurately.

42. **WTO (World Trade Organization)**: An international organization governing global trade, where blockchain could enhance compliance and efficiency in shipping.

43. **Smart Bill of Lading**: A digital version of the bill of lading stored on a blockchain, ensuring secure and efficient cargo documentation.

44. **Digital Twins**: Virtual models of physical assets, such as ships or cargo, used in conjunction with blockchain for better tracking and asset management.

45. **Carbon Tracking**: Monitoring of carbon emissions via blockchain to support sustainable shipping practices and compliance with environmental regulations.

46. **Blockchain Nodes**: Individual computers or servers that store copies of the blockchain ledger and validate transactions, used in decentralized shipping platforms.

47. **Electronic Data Interchange (EDI)**: The electronic transmission of data between shipping parties, which can be enhanced by blockchain for greater security.

48. **Blockchain Audits**: Reviews of transactions and records stored on a blockchain to ensure accuracy, compliance, and transparency in shipping.

49. **Permissioned Blockchain**: A type of blockchain where only authorized participants can validate transactions, commonly used in the shipping industry for privacy and security.

50. **Decentralized Applications (dApps)**: Applications built on blockchain that run on decentralized networks, potentially revolutionizing shipping operations.

www.ingramcontent.com/pod-product-compliance
Lightning Source LLC
Chambersburg PA
CBHW030041230526
45472CB00002B/622